GREATER GHOST

GREATER GHOST

Christian J. Collier

Four Way Books
Tribeca

For the Colliers & Hollingsheds:

the people that made me

Library of Congress Cataloging-in-Publication Data

Names: Collier, Christian J., 1983- author.
Title: Greater ghost / Christian Collier.
Description: New York : Four Way Books, 2024.
Identifiers: LCCN 2024000663 (print) | LCCN 2024000664 (ebook) | ISBN 9781961897106 (trade paperback) | ISBN 9781961897113 (epub)
Subjects: LCGFT: Poetry.
Classification: LCC PS3603.O447 G56 2024 (print) | LCC PS3603.O447 (ebook) | DDC 811/.6--dc23/eng/20240111
LC record available at https://lccn.loc.gov/2024000663
LC ebook record available at https://lccn.loc.gov/2024000664

This book is manufactured in the United States of America and printed on acid-free paper.

Four Way Books is a not-for-profit literary press. We are grateful for the assistance we receive from individual donors, public arts agencies, and private foundations including the NEA, and the New York State Council on the Arts, a state agency.

We are a proud member of the Community of Literary Magazines and Presses.

Contents

Boot Hill

I am soaked in my losses. My family's weight,
a royal gray gown wavering above me.
My husks slowly disappearing & falling into
gaps in the sod.

Where can one bury their skull & not hear,
in some direction, the cicada song of the living?

I turn my head to the left & see the future.
My yet-to-die are pollen-dusted.
My mama's mama is in the mahogany slats that appear
when I shut my eyes. Here,
I am in the kitchen watching her, up before the day—
the smell of breakfast filling the house
the city of Macon conned her out of.

She sinks a cube of butter into the navel of grits.
A pan of eggs—scrambled, salted & peppered to perfection—sits
on the coiled knuckle of a red burner.
The road bleeds slowly from the sky.
My uncles gather around her crowded ebony table—
eyes bloodshot, dry-rose lips starving for the day's first Newport.
We all ready ourselves to seal the meal inside our stomachs
by blessing both the food & the skilled hands that prepared it

1

& I say   speak, Lord,   tell me

      what is time but a shaky way
      to try to measure what can never be had back?
      A pore-ridden jar with which we attempt
      to recapture what has already gone its own way?
      What is nostalgia but another small demise, another way
      to slip through the deep black of a trapdoor's pupil?

Ghost [Retrograde]

I still touch myself   every few months
       to wake you,
          to bring you back to that night
where I bit the warm, wet ground on the brown edge of your thigh
as you sat atop the rosewood picnic table.

Your earth-scent in my nose,   salt & lacquer
behind the bell of my lips,   the church of you before me
         while I prayed
between the pillars of your knees.

You feel it   *don't you?*   Where you are now?   The rain,
the world around the pavilion bathed in downpour.
    The roof, a conga drum,
       a prestissimo tempo applauding on its metal jaw.

Beyond us, thunder sputtered in the distance.
Beyond us, one wobbly lamp flickered down the hill by the lake.
          Its constant blink,
    Morse code.
I didn't know it at the time, but it was prophesying,   saying
       hours after the weather cleared,
after we'd escaped back to our cars & left,   you would go
     silent,   then distant,   then gone.

No matter how many times I call you back, your last words remain pink noise. A plume of cool mist humming & coming apart over the slick back of tire-marked road.

In His Place

Somewhere beyond the window, wind drags its ghost
through the leaf-smudged trees.

It reaches in

to pull my face from the news of another Black man murdered.
This little wonder of nature,   the bullet
bringing my cousin back to me,   allowing

his voice
to pass from the paunch of one realm to the next

to tell me

I am on his mind.
I am on his mind.   I look up & don't find him,   discover
a silver rock dove sitting songless on a rain gutter's brow. It says,
If you want to see the wound, I will show you.
You can dip
your feathered hand

into the black pool of it. Its tide will climb
to dye your palm with grief. He extends
the sloped head of his wing,   changes
his mind,   leaps & becomes
a hurled stone gliding through

afternoon sky, leaves behind the truth
like a spent shell casing: mourning doesn't die.
    It's hunger ever-gnawing.
        The oily puddle of night that never leaves.

What Was Found

Instead of the little girl gone missing,
I found the carcass of a peacock
by the Blue Hole, frozen in the water.

Two arrows welded in the fat, teal tube of her neck.
A crystallized tear docked just below her open right eye.
In those woods, surrounded by chilled bark & branch,

> I wanted to tell her   *wake up.*
> I wanted to say   *fly with me.*
> I said   nothing.

I took a 40 oz. of Olde English to the head & poured a little out
to let the dead bird know
        she wasn't fully
            dead in me.

All she could remember was
still rooted on this side of living.
The coral blue god
who gave me this country
also gave a wealth of lifeless flesh to touch.

My steady brown hands,
at home in shed blood.   Sometimes,
I'm tired of the dead, the bulk of their mounting names.
Sometimes, I'm tired of trying
to keep the frost & rubble from their dying out.

Ghost [Tether]
for AJS

It's come to this.   Possession.
       She lives

in the screen of my computer now.
            Her spirit, one of the auburn lights pulsing

in the black box that doesn't sleep.
             I click the mouse & summon her face,

       then summon her name from my mouth.

    I say it   again   & again   & again

until the word becomes chorus & she has not passed on.
         I keep her breathing

    in this slight manner,
even though grief is a bruise-bodied, faceless god.

I know the dead hear everything,
       each day's example of how living wounds the living.

Early in the new morning, my blood remembers
                    they bury themselves

        inside us. They leave behind lean strands of arid soil
someone else is charged to worship.

            All I have of her to cradle are twenty-seven pictures,
                    twenty-seven square portals to moments

        she doesn't age beyond.   The past,
                    a blacklit ballroom

                        we wade into
        from different sides of an ebony curtain.

Lamentation

Loss is the language living pours between our teeth.
In a way, we are what sits between two broken bones.
That dilapidated space some pains stay pinned to.
Love, if you are a god, I pray for your favor.

In a way, we are what sits between two broken bones.
We died, too, but kept breathing.
Love, if you are a god, I pray for your favor.
If we must suffer, let it be as one.

We died, too, but kept breathing.
Where are we to go if the grave wants more of us?
If we must suffer, let it be as one.
How do we survive night, if not by faith the bone light will come?

Where are we to go if the grave wants more of us?
That dilapidated space some pains stay pinned to?
How do we survive night, if not by faith the bone light will come?
Loss is the language living pours between our teeth.

The Men in My Family Disappeared

behind horsefly-laden air & escaped the truth of the hearse.
We shot baskets in our black suits

before the funeral, the gospel was in the rumble of the missed shot
shivering off the backboard,

the soft moan of the free throws that fell
perfectly between the pursed lips of the rim.

Our laughter painted the dark-tinged sea between us, channeled
out from some urn inside the thicket of our organs.

I can't say if any of us knew where the body goes exactly
once it sifts through the salted colony of the skin, but I know

in the South, we sacred all we can to stay living, holy what is ours
before some rabid hand wrestles it away.

Beloved

We were riding the back end of a Charlotte thunderstorm, sailing
            through a galaxy of black & ash,
                    lightning   blooming briefly
                            around us,   when it struck me—

there isn't much difference between beauty & the ominous.

Then, as the five-year-olds behind me chanted about their hunger,

                    it occurred to me—

if God,   in His millennial pink Heaven above,   wished it so,
those dancing bolts could cleave the plane's abdomen & chuck us
                                        from the sky.

If that were to happen,   you would have sent me off
            into the unknown all souls someday arrive in, knowing
                    without question
                    I was loved.
            Wholly.
The way a famished fire washes over a building's flesh & marrow.
                    You baptized me
                even before I boarded.
                            You gave me

five white envelopes I folded & placed in my jacket pocket, each
                    containing
                    a letter
                    you penned
                    to remind me no matter where I went,
          no matter
if the plane plowed into some simple marvel of the earth,
    ending
                    all of us aboard
             in one deafening stroke,
I was divined by you.   Made angel already.

After the Bonfire

███████ when we downed your father's Jameson & smoked a bowl
on a patch of bent grass, emerald lightning below our skin,

I heard the gulf mumble to itself.
The words from its salt-filled mouth, reverberating.
It said it was tired of amassing
the names of lifeless things:
dented cans of Bud,   Marlboros,   bodies.

I felt the same way. I never told you, but it was all there.
In the almost silence,
our unwinged gods confess. Grief,
a splintered wooden raft, rollicking
always under the growling storms that won't relinquish us.
We wound & recover. Wound & recover.

I've never known
what becomes of us, the living, when
the gone we inherit are too many,   too onerous to still or hush.

It Follows

What more is there to say?
I don't want to make it about the 9mm round or the starless hour
██████'s heart caught the bullet & sagged, but

it broke through all the fine china in his chest.
It broke him down to the booze-drenched floorboards
when it ricocheted back out.

When he passed,
he transformed into something painted
in parched blood.   I couldn't draw him

back in my memory   without also inviting how
                he left me.
I'm already full of so much remembrance, so much smog & traffic
                on my road.

I'm a stone mausoleum at all times & wear those unable to
                                breathe with me.
It's always the things I can't hold onto that refuse to give me up,

always the things never meant to stay   that never leave.
        Anything unable to be escaped from is a prison.

Even the body.   Even being human.   Even being.
      This is the very nature of how a stain works—

one object marks & muddies another
      to the point where it'll never be made clean or whole again.
Beyond the surface of a thing,   it punctures past the white meat.
          The wound remains an open border.

Wolf River

On all that has left me, I swear
that water is a religion anyone can bend into & emerge unsaved.

I steer clear of its pulse, the gravity below its chisel-gray allure.
I can't face the brine you drowned in.

Your homegoing poisoned it. I know
                              the breath,

the last balloon of fire winnowed from you, is docked in its sway.
Your ghost—tealed, bloated—is bound to me now. She says

there is a field of alabastrine deer who wear dust-made capes
at the edge of this living.

                  I want to believe
                              you suffer no more.

I want a sign you still exist, one strum of a major chord, but you,
                  you keep dead.

                  That's the problem.

The Compline

Between us, there are one hundred one
umber haints in our home.

In bed, we discuss
our future, our children woven in myrrh, sitting

in some tomorrow, waiting for us to join & give them our science
so they can live.

I tell her what I fear: I'll walk into fogged, writhen woods & die
when our babies are too young to carry my baritone with them.

I'll become
the almost-stranger

they hear their mother's prayers paint the night sky for.
The Lord giveth & The Lord taketh parents every day.

Love is no shield against His mighty ginger hand or will.
Even language passes away.

Even the bouquet of vowels & syllables collected
each year can be swept from the scaly floor of the tongue.

All stories end in death
if we are honest with ourselves & how the world works.

If I am being honest,
when I, eventually, hear my love sleeping by my side,

I eye the gloom, whisper to God,   ask that He spare me
the escape, the emptying out of the marigold light,

for many years. I ask that, when it finally comes, I not go before
I know all I've set my heart upon will live on well without me.

I ask Him to forgive my selfish maw for having the nerve
to call out His name & flood His holy ear with the word   *more.*

In the Spectral Hour

At the foot of her hospital bed,   I became my mama's god
while she was sick, battling infection

I wondered, as I struggled to keep her fed & in minimal pain,
who would keep her safe when she left me
if she crossed over before my hazel eyes

Who would walk with her
to the bronze palace where all souls sleep

Whose hands would part the alarm-thick air & usher her over
the thin, damp threshold of this plane & into the honeyed light

When she threw up after eating
for the first time in three days, I thought of how
   my grandmother told her my cousin came to visit

My cousin, who died, arrived & said
   he would soon return to take her
      between the pearl-rimmed stars
         She could abandon her worry
           I wanted that to be the way it works for everyone—

the slow fade into soundlessness,
the hushing of lamps

I wanted to ask if she feared what was coming—the changing
of the scene, the slimming of the leaves, the softening of the meat
for forever's consumption   I swallowed the notion

Whenever my mama talked,
    I watched the shade draw closer,   each step, making her vanish

Ghost [Talisman]

In a naked world flanked by bare trees & bush,
I stood in a shower of snow behind the old building I worked in.
The black branches of my beard painted white.
My face hovered above the cell phone screen. Waiting. Waiting.
Then, you arrived in a picture, unthreaded,
wearing only lamplight. The warm ivory patch of country beneath
your belly button held a golden gleam.
You, wherever you were in the region, fed me flesh
& made a fanged, hirsute thing of me.
Like a man hearing the voice of man's maker the first time,
you locked my limbs in place. Caged me.
If only you could've heard the sigh you worked from my pores
without knowing. Without notice.
How my feral vox fell musicless after.
If only you could've felt the tremor, the stars unknit from my gut.
If only you hadn't disappeared,
I would tell you what I have told no one.
I swallowed all I could of you that day,
every bit I could keep down.

I Was a Ferry among the Stars

When the wind walked me up & down Rossville Ave.,
██████████, I wore the yellow shirt you bled out in
& brought us everywhere.
I made my rounds as a starling
in this city some dead never return to.
I carried the three syllables of your name
in the open fields between my teeth
along with broken leaves & bits of wood. Each letter,
a pile of sand lime bricks. You lived

in my star-rubbed breast & nowhere else.
The buried never stop arriving
in small words. The buried never stop reminding me
we have forever & not enough hours
to call the salt of one another home.
I grow full, then made empty again.
This is everything I know of family, the treasured blood & spirit.

I keep the days from ending
by not allowing the sepia men who look like me to wilt.
I never know abandon
when it comes to my fallen.
I shove my curled toes into humid air & feel closer to every one.

I know the Lord's low voice, His plainsong,
through all I refuse to waste.

Leaving the Earth

As we gallop down the runway & scale cloud-peppered sky,
I chant the seven names of my airborne dead & feel them close.
      They see me shudder
at the thought of becoming one of them, the unbreathing. I admit:
I never get nearer to God than when I wish not to join Him.

         My God,
I hate leaving any party before I'm ready,
before I've had my fill of white rum or cake.
I'm not prepared for the doors to shut & lock.
I've so loved this sun-groomed globe,
each minute bit I've been served,
I fear letting go, being snagged from it
like a sailfish   snared through the mouth & yanked
from its saltwater bath.   My brother told me long ago
there is no Heaven, but, instead, an indigo hole, a grand nothing
awaiting each of us once we've run out of clocks.
I have never learned what to do with time—
the days archived, the shelled portion of hours I have left
in the taut canvas around my belly.

I don't know how anybody dies easy,
how they reach willingly for the starlit ladder,
how they do it without a protest bluing their tongue.

I am afraid
I don't know how to go anywhere
      calm-blooded.
All I know is how not to be slain or make any room
        I enter   a man-made shrine
to house my corpse.

Benediction for the Black & Young

Children, we occupy a planet not made to carry any of us.
            Find the slivers of calm
      in the ash-filled air.   Breathe.
Do you feel the atoms
      coming apart around the garlic-white brims of our halos?

We are living through a time that took touch   from us,
      wading through the stubble of the burning night,
            finessing our feet forward   as best we can.

                  Let us pray
                  there is a just God

                  at the end of all of this.   Let us pray
            He sees the columns of our dead
on the sour buds of the street, pray He stirs & says *enough*.

      Let us pray
the booze that drags us from one day to the next doesn't run out,
            pray the Hennessy & Crown stays put,

      pray we do the same sane & intact. Let us lay down our blues
& not cross the threshold of another morning howling
            for those we could not see buried.

Let us pray
for the favor of the big sky, for burgundy wings no longer tucked
                    beneath our shoulders & a sheath
        below the twitch of the stars.

Let us bow our heads & dream
a life that loves us better.   May it be gold-hued.

        May our minds sculpt a love supreme that also holds
our newborn ghosts.   Let us whisper, because history says
        whenever someone Black wonders aloud about
            the future, it instantly becomes a bruised sea of days
                    they'll never know.
Children,
if we are only meant to forfeit
all that has ever known our names,
let us fraternize with
the condors who'll come to escort us away.
Let the stomp of our forelimbs be
the last bit of grace
we grant this land.

                    Then, let us rest well.
                        Let us be.

Alchemy

The city breathed around us when we learned
we were going to be parents

                                        Did you feel it

When each aging inch of us became a harbinger of new life
You belonged to the oldest, most-hallowed coven ever known

In the late night's hush, I heard drumming—
the crimson machinery coiled within you   at work building
                 a portal
for our child to pass through

On the Midnight Hike

A gray fox sat frozen
on a patch of grassless clod,
seventy-three ivory pebbles

scattered around her, a congregation of teeth sleeping on the trail,
white as the sliced & open stomach of an apple.
The syrup moon illuminated her shoulders & scalp.

Her eyes, soft hazel lights, dreadless,
watching me standing
a few yards away

on the sloped black lobe of a boulder.
Thinking you would enjoy this scene, this beauty,
██████████, I raised my phone,   took a picture,   texted it to you.

                I forgot
                you are dead now.
I remembered you, not the rests the grave tucked inside your jaw.

            I couldn't say
how I lost, even briefly, the memory: the soil torn open for you;
the gape shivering to be filled with your oak coffin;

the mute swans sobbing
in the creamrose clouds.
      I want to know

     how could I have been that flawed in mind,   that human
amid so much wild?

Passport

The American beech trees are balding.
The February sky is a leaden sleeve.
The ground, muddy.

Everything is wet & alone.

Everything untouched shivers,
beautiful in its exposure, when
a bluebird delivers a minor-keyed dirge
through the jagged hole a predator left in her nest
when it snagged & killed her lover.

I, too, pine in the open for my dead
when I feel nothing else is watching or close enough to hear.

I, too, have been a winged, damaged gorge
singing out to a careless wind.

Sanctuary

When I believed my mother was dying   in a tiny hospital bed,
I went to the only place in Chattanooga one could watch
        topless women dance for money.

I sought the refuge of a body—exposed & illuminated, a trapdoor
      to escape   the body—   seemingly failing & falling.
My hands gripped her breathing tube, placed it

        back into her nostrils,
then clutched crinkled dollar bills   & hurled them
  on the scuffed scalp of the stage,   each green & weathered one

                                a piece of her patient gown
      a wraith was rolling
                  between its hidden fingers.

Dead Time

It was a horrible dream
        for a moment
when you called & said   in a slight   tattered   voice

                      you lost the baby
            When I realized it
was true, not something merciless a bad connection fed me—

    the blue spark that originated
  in me & settled in the soil within
      you had fallen black

because some titan we'd never know or see had cut it down
    every organ inside the kiln of my round stomach collapsed
        I heard no other word you breathed, cannot recall replying

to assure you we'd be okay when I was uncertain we could be
When it registered I couldn't be there to layer myself around you
        I became undead & traipsed to the liquor store

across the street from the hotel I was spending the night in
  I wanted white fire & found my lips around a bottle of Ketel One
    I swallowed down all it offered   quickly   without pleasure

like a man possessed by   the need to feel nothing

What I Know to be True

Weeks later, I was rearrested
when I watched the video.

The camera's silent stare captured the last seconds of peace.
On the morning my mother told me of the murder,

a pigeon on the asphalt burst like a glass globe,
a red & gray world rubbled

at my feet. The earth failed me, gave me
no warning of its news.

The wind held no death in its yawn.
The orbs of water that lined the soil didn't taste of copper

before the bleeding out.
I found my mouth on the verge of crying

for him to take cover
as if it would have mattered,

as if it would have altered a goddamn thing & spared me.
There is a part of me that does not want my cousin to rest,

it wants him to reside in his murderer & murder him
one memory at a time

while he faces
the same set of concrete prison walls   day in,   day out.

Even when I want
no more ruin, no more

death, to be freed from
its absolute work, I yearn for his.

This is what the killing's done, caused me to want
my loved & lost

made a bludgeon for the man whose stray shot slumped
my bloodline.

Aubade in a Time of Stillness

When my mother was mending
after surgery,   I was the air between two lovers.

In one cramped bed, one small TV's lone teal light blanketed us.
We cooled & dried against each other

as snow remade West 20th Street
beyond the window.   The Southside was silent.

No gun screamed a death song up or down the block.
Under the shed & magic of that clouded panoply,

we tongued enough of the good time to survive the blue hour.
The winter would've wrongly sworn, had it peered inside,

we shared a pulse that sewed us together,
some sort of love that sealed us,   thigh to thigh.

What we had, though,   only a borrowing
before we gave ourselves up & never spoke again.

We are, all of us,   made not to last
in one another or anywhere.

We are always in the life of, at least,   one kind of dying.
The intimate passes through the atoms as a pant.

We pass through one another, then,   out the door
long before the rust sets in.

The Day of the Funeral

We become nameless together,
transform for a swell of hours into   *the family.*
               The left behind.   *The grieving.*

On this day, we give your child
the world that took you from her, everything
we try to hope better.
Not a trail of ugly hours to cry into,
a litany of purpled skies no peach-winged beast has touched.

Look at how we weep to keep from drowning, from filling
to the point of rupture on the gristle of this sadness.

Look at how we say goodbye, how we lug your murder around
in the creak of our clinched jaws.

We've gathered to give you to the earth to keep track of,
the soot-faced gods in the minerals commit you to the bed of soil
               beneath us,
the soiled bed God & Death made for you.
We are counting the minutes until it holds you.

God

I used to think
there was only one of You
before the miscarriage.
Now, I am not so sure.
Maybe there are a number of Gods to wade through
before falling at the feet of the last true one:

      the jade God we pray to
      who does not come or answer
      & the plum one who appears to offer salvation;
      the opal God who offers a limited extent of His kingdom
      & the olive one who only offers condolences;
      let us not forget the violet God that is bad with man
      because He is deeply holy.

We all seek the one of manna though, don't we?
He, the one of follow-through.
He, the one of action & consequence.
He, the one holding all we hunger for
like butterscotch in His palms.

That's the God I want
to be alone with for a few moments,
the God I wish to have to myself

in the hushed hours when I should be up & readying for work
like millions of other souls dispersed
across the country's ink-black pillow.

That's the God whose name I utter
when I sit in silence
on the shoulder of my mattress. I dream
with eyes open of goading Him into halting my child's rest,
guiding his or her tiny light close to the brushfire
flickering in my breath.

That God? *That* great & swollen orange storm?
That's the God haunting me.   The God who keeps His distance.
The God whose star-draped hands I envy.
They come at day's end
to tuck my baby, my ember, into its infinite, feathered bed.

The Return

A funeral brought me back to church
after several years
away from the golden crosses & groaning pews.
I sat in the balcony,
an auburn leaf in the slim cradle of a rain gutter,
staring down at the shut black coffin, imagining
the body of my friend
underneath the heavy lid—

this body   a vacant cave,
this body   a stranger,   a foreign continent.

Behind the casket,
the members of the choir blended their voices.
I thought of this body's young, resting face—

the cheeks, now thinner, loose;
the lips, now dry & permanently bound.
A hiss, somewhere in the garden inside my skull, said,

He is no longer here & where he has gone, you cannot yet follow.

I closed my eyes momentarily & realized
this was death's work,   segregating

the living
who are still dying & made to stay behind.

The Ritual

I have never been one who truly believed
in the act of resurrection,

someone or something that has passed veining
          back into its body   for more life.

I abandoned the belief long ago of who I once was ever returning
to inhabit this flesh again,

convinced, for the rest of my days,
he'll be frozen in a wall of glass & live on only as a specter,

a refracted memory stranded
in my recollection.

Even though it defies all logic,
          even though I know better,

          I still devote a portion of each day attempting
to breach time & space

in order to breathe him back into me,
          or, just breathe being back into him,

pass enough air & wheat light into the trench of his throat
to wake him from the grave he's been sleeping in.

I know no matter how ardently I want
      to begin again,

to touch the smooth fabric of his honey skin & revel in its newness,
      he is gone forever, the ghost who'll never come

to haunt the brittling bones housed within me.

Sauna

The white towel covering me knows
     I am afraid of death,   yes,   of tripping   out of life

                   beyond the speckled dark.
  I taste a little bit of the grave   each time
my chest muscles tighten & the next breath   stands
        a mile beyond me.   I am afraid of the day
my lips could   reach for   & only latch onto
      the three blank shells
of   an ellipses.

      I know what it is to go   without   & I am afraid
I don't know what   squander means
             when it comes to   respiration.
I live ever in search   of oxygen   & waste none I find.
   Asthma   is the name   of what eats away at me—
           thief of the lungs
that could one day rob me   of you.
         Breath is   a temporary beast
   a frightened deer   sometimes sprinting
away &   out of view   I tame

by forming a refuge from steam.
       That boneless dancer   only knows

surrender,   only answers to
                        the wild flow of its limbs.
    I inhale,   then cleave to
the apparitions birthed by this heat
                        I   invite them inside me
                in order to breathe,
    in order to not go   dead   among the living.

Ghost [Communion]

I lost my appetite for so many things
                                        after you died.

Something inside couldn't bring itself
                    to crave the taste of salt or sugar.

        When I awakened,
I belonged to myself again.

                                    What unlatched within me
to relight the praying candles that had fallen dark?

        I came to be released on a wrinkled pile of bedsheets,
to open myself & be touched by a bawd's detached palms.

            I came for her to sanctify me,
her hands upon my pelvis,   as if she loved me.

    We were strangers, our real names hearsed
                in the hollows of our mandibles.

                            I can't say how desire bloomed
                in the mineral of my bones.

I was comfortable   venturing into the late hour
to glance skyward & find a glimpse of God

       in the gray naps of the popcorn ceiling—
sacrificing my divine future, my forever

       as an offering.
    Pleasure rung out of me,   a thrum

from a bronze church bell's mouth.

In the Blood

When something dies,   everything dies.
   The chilled wind heaves itself haggardly through the gash left
in the galled walls of the abdomen. No one says

      the limping heart decays into an ugly warehouse of emotion
when you're truly tarred. No one says how to rebuild, revise
      the woe sitting cyst-like in the muscles.

Silence makes its own score. We've slowly worked to eat into it,
   to hear ourselves exhale again. In the dark,   in the blind heat,
it was kismet. We found one another & touched to endure, to feel.

We called upon the deities in the blush of our nerves & hands,
            return us to the world we struggled to recognize,
      the world we barely fit into with a bend in its winking stars.

In the Time of Dying, Meet Me

Father of mass & air pressure,
turbulent altitude & dewed skyline.
If these burgundy wings carrying me across
Your vulture-strewn puce road should weaken, should fail,
please   descend with me.   Just once
borrow a tenor & talk
to make my plummet an easy sprint toward sea sand floor.

Bend low Your busy ear so my last asks of You land intact.
My uncle, King Cobra on his breath, once said
anyone who stays in the wind too long never leaves it behind.
Let it be true. Let me be
both here & not here completely.
Let some of me be nine black hickory leaves jitterbugging
on the proud curving lip of any given gust.

Let me be story, in that way,
when these tensed lungs struggle no more or work.
When I am man no longer,
new in shape, beyond blood & gland,
let my uttered name be a blue note lanterning my loves' voices

from time to time. Anoint what red dirt of me is left
through hymn. Father, let me be occasional music   after shh.

Blood

The last word my love speaks before we hang up becomes
a sustained G sharp   in my head until, next door,   I hear
water, running as if down & over the smooth backs of
several stones the size of a child's skull & in its song,
my grandmother's voice crests
the percussion, says, *Come with me* & we are both in stride,
the divots in our palms now small ponds
as we walk across the sodden collar of the grass
above the casket where she sleeps.

I ask if it was true
she once put a bullet in my grandfather
for keeping time with another woman.

She says,   *Yes,*
                    & I'd do it again.

I step into a slight hollow,
the water slips through my fingers & becomes fresh polish
upon the turf. I apologize.

I ask if I've disappointed her by not being more alert. She says,
     I've seen the secrets you keep as railroad ties
beneath your tongue. I love you the same as I always have.

When I mention *my love*, my wish
she was alive to meet her, she says,

I already have.

What you don't understand is,
my life begins again
every day you offer up the hymn of your breath.
Baby, we are blood &

blood is the oldest god
any of us can look to & always find—
the gospel of this is something
time can never touch, the good news that does not die.

Monologue to an Oatmeal Moon

Let me sing to you of what happened
right before you stumbled upon your throne.

The wind dipped its hand into the back of the lake & stirred
a spell I couldn't look away from.

The beauty broke me from the unwonder of
the current time that killed my friend.   As I stared on

in reverence, one mosquito gruffly taxied through
the evening's peach crescendo

& left with a piece of me,
my blood, in its throat.

That slight beast did   the most male & American of acts, thieved
what belonged to me without consent.

Now, a sliver of my legacy has had to erect
a tent in a new earth's gut amid a torrent of acids & spectres.

That quick kiss caused
the instruments of the near-night

to unfurl me,   sent a stream of
what has gone missing sweeping by—

its scent,   stroking the cavern of my nostrils.
I wondered, as the drum roll from

its wings grew more mute
each second it escaped beyond me,

if this was what intimacy meant now
in the era of the longed-for touch.

        Interveniente,
one virus clamoring to replace the maraud of another

& either way,
my body belongs not wholly to itself,

my body becomes taken treasure, a means
to sate something else's need to be fed. This is nothing new.

Consumption is always what becomes of the body
if it exists in the wild long enough.

My body is always in season
to be mashed by the teeth of one being or another

that is tired of dining only on dark air.
Dear inflamed, ovaled moon,

do you know how filled with want I'd been
before that black bug's tiny sting?   How strongly

I'd been thirsting   for something breathing to taste me?
When his mouth heard me & wallowed in my sweet & salt,

I didn't once think to raise my hands & clap the life out of him.
I combed the bridge of my palm over the shade he drank from

attempting to close the short doors he left stranded open   when
he pulled his slender lips away from me.

Mercutio

I knew the wound ran deeper than I let on
when it first appeared, but
I kept the truth in
as long as I could.

I carried the horror & wore it in such a manner
no one knew where I'd been or what had been taken from me.
When I could sprint no longer or stay beyond its reach,
my damage brought me wholly into its den & pinned me.
The ground's green breast burned any reserve I'd been clinging to
before my eyes. Everything chambered between
the moon-hued planks of my vertebrae bellowed
& loped into the open.

I became someone else, someone perforated & new
who, for the first time, cursed God
as well as the demon that thieved the child from my lover & me.

I clasped my hands, asked any other deity that could hear me
to cast a plague that would shrapnel both their houses.

Case Study

We were ravaged   by our loss,   our child.
        In the shower,   slightly past midnight,
after I'd covered the length & width of her back with suds,

        she started crying.   Then,   I started crying.
The grief we could no longer cradle, a house sparrow's song,
        poured from us   into a bundle of steam.

        Our slumped network of nerves & muscle convulsed
                                while we bawled.
We stood in limbo, beyond time,

a faint gray comma
        between us & the planet rotating beside
our flesh. The shower tiles drank us in,

                their unblinking, marble eyes absorbed
what becomes of two poisoned creatures
        when their future, each sage green branch of it, has died back.

The Morning After

Our hammers ushered the song of men
at work with their hands & treated wood
                    into the day. With each solid jab,
        the platoon of pulled nails in the mouth of my pouch chanted.
Mosquitoes hovered around my skin, carrying their appetites
                        like arrows in a quiver.
                        All of this—
                the humid morning air, the dense xeric heat,
        the ache-drenched back, knees, arms–was mine,
                    a contractor's gifts. The tree
branches above cut the sunlight into a million & one jewels
                    the morning after you were killed.

Glory Box

After we made love the first time
atop the whine of my old mattress,
I filled the room with the slow swell & strut
                   of Portishead's "Glory Box."

Beth Gibbons delicately crooned the first seven words
in the chorus to some faceless, nameless being. Perhaps

those lyrics wedged inside you, your yellow marrow
interpreting them as a quest born quietly that day.

In the years that have followed,
you've granted reason after reason
to pin the rough, maroon fabric of my heart to the wall of yours.

You have allowed me to believe
time & again
you're the one the cherry canopy of my soul should forever shelter.

Precious Lord

After all these years, You still have a sense of humor.
How could I not look back & laugh at the irony of it all?
How could I not appreciate the perfection of the timing?

When I had decided not to die, I almost did.
I still picture his face—
the blonde boy
behind the wheel   who didn't see me
until it was too late.

I called out Your name
as I sat still & bloodied in my driver's seat
attempting to piece together what happened.

A Venetian Red sun ducked behind a bundle of asphalt clouds.
My cut, parched mouth gasped,
if not for air, then something, anything, near that tasted like life.

Submission

Beneath the crepe plateau of my tongue

I've made sure to keep the truth an ivory pearl entombed

My body has become a cemetery, a steel safe unable to let go
Surrender means letting our lost one that ashen bit of us die again

I said it

before I meant it

███████ , I told you I'd moved beyond the miscarriage before I had

Tell me
how exactly

does one journey away from these ruins, step outside them

Each morning my reflection reminds me

I am the maker of a cerulean light not meant for life
I've lost count how many times
I've sat on the edge of our moaning bed   wondering

which one of our intimate exchanges set this in motion

which sunless hour
did I descend inside you & plant what would have been our child

First Time After

The first time we made love after the miscarriage,
she wailed, locked herself
     in the bathroom when we finished. She filled it with sobs.
The hardest thing, knowing what sealed her
               in there, the miry feelings,
knowing she had to abide them alone.

     She was coming to terms with all of it—
our little shine's absence, the rediscovery of joy, her very body.
          From our ruffled bed, it dawned on me—
time is a god unto itself. Stubborn, but giving.
     Its wide hands heal when they're ready, not when we'd like, no,
not when we're in need's flame-filled middle, pleading for rescue.

     The act of healing hurts until it fades from both bone & mind,
someday, if we're fortunate.
     When she exited with cold, fresh water gleaming on her face,
I held her, rested my damp head against hers
          as she pretended
she hadn't been wrenched open & felt
     the toll of two worlds at once.

When My Days Fill with Ghosts

When my days fill with ghosts, there are corpses
on the streets of New York. Ambulance song in the air
every few minutes. I'm groundless when a friend tells me
████████ is dead. I keep thinking of his three sons,
how his low voice now exists only in memory.

*

████████ is dead.
I watch the last few seconds of his life
in landscape mode on my cell phone.
I know, then, I have had enough.
I can never willingly see the end for anyone else Black.
I am too full on death to want to witness any more.

*

████████ is dead because of the police.
I haven't breathed deeply since February.
I haven't let a night pass without crossing myself,
begging God to intervene.

*

Holy, the spirits.

      Holy, the Grey Goose,

the Elijah Craig Small Batch.

      Holy, the Patrón that awakens

the burn in my throat, my chest, my liver.

      Holy, the touch that brings,

for a moment, the bite of something more than dread.

*

The fever comes one summer night.

Unsure if this is regular sickness or the sickness that killed ███████,

I imagine my life without me.

After I sweat through the cotton bedsheets,

I tell the swaying shadows

I'm afraid to live air-hungry, then not at all.

*

      The next morning,

I take the interstate into Georgia

& don't think about where to stop or turn around.

I commit everything the neon sun holds to my blood
in case the dark comes in the next two weeks.

*

After   my   ██████   dies,
my   ██████   tells   me
my   ██████   can't   stop   sobbing.
I   don't   hear   him,
knowing   he   is   mourning   unknits   me.
I   don't   remember
the   last   time   he's   been   this   exposed,   this   human.

*

Hours after I bend my knee
& ask my love to marry me,   my ██████ dies.
I am afraid to cry, to open myself, to give any emotion

to this barbed, new world.
I fear the release, the emptiness, if it all oceans out.

*

    The   year   ends
with fireworks in the distance & Johnnie Walker Black Label
        in a Styrofoam cup. The year ends.
My dead are still gone. The year ends.
I've yet to stop feeling the roots dying beneath my feet.

Acknowledgments

Many thanks to the judges and editors who chose these poems for publication. They appeared for the first time, sometimes in an earlier version, in the following:

The American Journal of Poetry, Atlanta Review, December, Grist: A Journal of the Literary Arts, Hayden's Ferry Review, Michigan Quarterly Review, North American Review, Poet Lore, The Seven Hills Review, Sinew: 10 Years of Poetry in the Brew, 2011-2021, Symposium, Timber, and *The Wild Word.*

The utmost love and gratitude to the following for supporting me and making this work possible:

Curtis and Cheryl Collier, Caitlin Collier, Dr. Cayanna, AJ, Julianna, and Antwan Good, James McKissic, Rebecca Palmer, Tyree Daye, Vievee Francis, Donna Spruijt-Metz, Detroit Nick Makouske, Marcus Thomas, Christine Hall, Byron Staples, Sybil Baker, Isaac Duncan, Richard Winham, Ronda Foster, Judith Sachsman, Bao Phi, Wess Mongo Jolley, Ray Bassett, Adera Causey, Artsbuild, RISE Chattanooga, The Loft Literary Center, The University of Tennessee at Chattanooga, WUTC, Scenic Trend, The Plug Poetry Project, Ross White, Noah Stetzer, Cassie Mannes Murray, Shawnessey Cargile, and everyone at Four Way Books.

Love eternal to:

Carolyn Alford
Marco Collins
Annie Laura Neal Hollingshed
Corey Hollingshed Jr.
Linda Hollingshed
Sam Howard
Taurus Kelley
Andrew Kelsay
Florida Morris
Pamela Sims
Amber Jaime Sorenson
Raymond Stewart
Cynthia Wild-Joyner

About the Author

Christian J. Collier is a Black, Southern writer, arts organizer, and teaching artist who resides in Chattanooga, Tennessee. He is the author of *Greater Ghost* (Four Way Books, 2024) and the chapbook *The Gleaming of the Blade*, the 2021 Editors' Selection from Bull City Press. His works have appeared in *December, Hayden's Ferry Review, North American Review, The Michigan Quarterly Review,* and elsewhere. A 2015 Loft Spoken Word Immersion Fellow, he is also the winner of the 2022 Porch Prize in Poetry and the 2020 ProForma Contest from *Grist Journal*. More about him and his work can be found at www.christianjcollier.com

We are also grateful to those individuals who participated in our Build a Book Program. They are:

Anonymous (14), Robert Abrams, Debra Allbery, Nancy Allen, Michael Ansara, Kathy Aponick, Jean Ball, Sally Ball, Jill Bialosky, Sophie Cabot Black, Laurel Blossom, Tommye Blount, Karen and David Blumenthal, Jonathan Blunk, Lee Briccetti, Jane Martha Brox, Mary Lou Buschi, Anthony Cappo, Carla and Steven Carlson, Robin Rosen Chang, Liza Charlesworth, Peter Coyote, Elinor Cramer, Kwame Dawes, Michael Anna de Armas, Brian Komei Dempster, Renko and Stuart Dempster, Matthew DeNichilo, Rosalynde Vas Dias, Patrick Donnelly, Charles R. Douthat, Lynn Emanuel, Blas Falconer, Laura Fjeld, Carolyn Forché, Helen Fremont and Donna Thagard, Debra Gitterman, Dorothy Tapper Goldman, Alison Granucci, Elizabeth T. Gray Jr., Naomi Guttman and Jonathan Meade, Jeffrey Harrison, KT Herr, Carlie Hoffman, Melissa Hotchkiss, Thomas and Autumn Howard, Catherine Hoyser, Elizabeth Jackson, Linda Susan Jackson, Jessica Jacobs, Deborah Jonas-Walsh, Jennifer Just, Voki Kalfayan, Maeve Kinkead, Victoria Korth, David Lee and Jamila Trindle, Rodney Terich Leonard, Howard Levy, Owen Lewis and Susan Ennis, Eve Linn, Matthew Lippman, Ralph and Mary Ann Lowen, Maja Lukic, Neal Lulofs, Anthony Lyons, Ricardo Alberto Maldonado, Trish Marshall, Donna Masini, Deborah McAlister, Carol Moldaw, Michael and Nancy Murphy, Kimberly Nunes, Matthew Olzmann and Vivee Francis, Veronica Patterson, Patrick Phillips, Robert Pinsky, Megan Pinto, Kevin Prufer, Anna Duke Reach, Paula Rhodes, Yoana Setzer, James Shalek, Soraya Shalforoosh, Peggy Shinner, Joan Silber, Jane Simon, Debra Spark, Donna Spruijt-Metz, Arlene Stang, Page Hill Starzinger, Catherine Stearns, Yerra Sugarman, Arthur Sze, Laurence Tancredi, Marjorie and Lew Tesser, Peter Turchi, Connie Voisine, Susan Walton, Martha Webster and Robert Fuentes, Calvin Wei, Allison Benis White, Lauren Yaffe, and Rolf Yngve.